Girls and Boys in Water

Rhosalyn Williams

Boys and Girls in Water ©2020 by **Rhosalyn Williams**. Published in the United States by Vegetarian Alcoholic Press. Not one part of this work may be reproduced without expressed written consent from the author. For more information, please contact vegalpress@gmail.com

Cover art by Kate Divoll

Eve Shovels A Grave...3

A Fish in Me...4

Girl As I Was...6

Rebirth, After The Last Time...7

Enough Sun...8

Upon Hearing Female Dragonflies Fake Their Own Deaths to Avoid Males, I Consider Wendy Peffercorn...9

Cul-De-Sac Queen...11

The Local Boys...12

The Holding Pond...13

Nautical Astronomy...14

Bad Dog, Come Back...15

Even...16

I Bring The Body To Work In...17

Who's The Bitch?...18

One Last Thing...19

Sea Witch...20

I'm Telling You Ma...21

When I Go Down...22

Homecoming...23

for Florida

Eve Shovels A Grave

And you're young too, but you stopped
picking smooth-skinned fruit years ago
and you don't watch me anymore—

So I get low to the earth
and feel around for something ripe.
The trees, so far and high,
are sporting God, His grey belly hair
mixed in with the Spanish moss,
His dreams sopping the roots.

You, alone,
asleep with your eyes open all night, you
caught the moon in your craw.

So I split a pomegranate
and like to see the knife come back
wet, red.

I promise I'm young
and I still like the flesh.

A Fish In Me

Mother! Then
I was gasping, dying
I thought, and you said
Dad was a bastard
to let me wail so long.
Remember, you took
the fishbone out of me?
You said I was a mermaid then,
and pulled the long tangles
out of my hair. Kitten,
you called me. Sweet,
here's a piece of ice
to roll in your mouth.

Your palm on my back,
the flat sound,
the wet heave--
and between it I could hear
the living thing thrashing in me.

I listened to it as it
travelled in me: I felt it
in my knee crook,
it kissed me in the chest.

After you took it I swallowed one more.
It wanted a fish hook,
It wanted scales;
It sang into a beer bottle;
Swam the English Channel.

Mermaid, you called me,
Big Girl--
        Will you cut your hair
        in your other life?

What will happen
if I do?

I will love you,
        you said.

Less and less, you said,
        but I will love you.

Girl As I Was

On the drive, I look out a little ways to watch
the yellow hills worked along
by a girl with her shirt off, like the girl I was

between the woods and the earth under,
before my body
           became too much for bearing. I speed up
             to get past her, burning all the gas I can manage,
                  until she could be a billy goat, gnawing.

Why always this need
           to hold on?
How then,
           I fed my stomach round on everything
and my soft hand. Hideous indulgence that burns
'till she's gone, so she can never look up
           and see

the way I've given up my long hair, the belt
           so tight against my chest, I'm choking.

But here's the dog to be taken out and shot.
And I know that by now, she's pissed
everywhere she shouldn't. No more of this
backward mind, only
the long,
           straight route.

Rebirth, After The Last Time

Into the stitched belly of Mother
for all the distress I have caused her,
I will crawl back, burrow back,
into the easy caw of mourning—
the first breath breathed back, returned to me,
smalling my lungs, crippling the expanse of all
I have left on Her spirit.

Of all my twenty digits, I will have none.
Coil back into myself and have life through my navel,
not as a bird or a fish, gasping stupidly
at the filthy stuff of earth.
Instead, blink blindly, smaller, smaller.
No more this scalding on my back,
never me in Her stolen white skirt,
worn out of the streetlamps, unlost—

Meanwhile, me, suckling on a stump.
Warm and unnamed, only the soft impression
of Her hand every once in a while, little gurgles, coos.

After all that went wrong: the van, 2 AM
siren call of my father, crushed, and me,
who I led out of the woods with a scout knife…

There is still no answer on the other end.
And She will have so little memory of me
as to keep living, eyes set ahead
on the sun, exactly and forever
at noon.

Enough Sun

Can it be this week
that the moon sat so long and large in the sky
as I swung dirty achilles?

The radio described a man
"blue" and "bloody" in Lavernock Bay
and I had cake and my mother on the phone.
People keep talking. And I listen,
like a tic.

"I'm not trying to put boots on a caterpillar,"
the customer said
"I just wanna fuck." He got my number.

Certainly, it was this week
that Roy Moore stood on stage and pulled
a pistol from his pants; he pulled
the pistols from his pants. The audience
existed with or without the sound
turned on! It was only a photo-op
in the end. It was this week,
I'm certain.

I heard sweeter things went on abroad.
I heard a child like Michael slept well
in the bunk the Unicef ad bought him,
he is asleep with his mouth open
and a very good God
drops pennies into his heart.

Upon Hearing Female Dragonflies Fake Their Own Deaths to Avoid Males, I Consider Wendy Peffercorn

Wendy saw Squints dying and went down
for a breath. A poor glittering fish,
he pulled up quiet from the water.
She prodded his belly with an acrylic nail
and the nail sunk and the flesh
sprung back, but the boy didn't start
coughing.

In the corner already,
someone is composing a eulogy.
Remembered for nothing in particular,
it isn't long.

Wendy listens for a heart. Something inside
must be telling her to move to the mouth and she,
blonde hair taken by the wind behind her,
leans down, 14, blows hot air into his mouth.

She imagines that he is a pool float.
She imagines that this is practice, and the smell
of his mouth is new plastic instead of bacteria
and death.

She's gone for his heart again
and in the interim, her head
on his stomach, the dead thing winks.

And the stillness of his limbs
and the quiet of the boys
allow the dead to be dead, or nearly.

And Wendy is mouth to his mouth again,
and his hands, so well-behaved, shift into
her hair, her tanned shoulders--

Wendy paints her toes
fire-engine red on the arm
of the lifeguard stand.

From her tower, Wendy watches
rows of dead boys,

come to fall at her feet.

Cul-De-Sac Queen

The boy who lived next door had no father. So his mother was stern and quiet. In our garage, Dad let him practice with power tools, but the boy didn't have an interest. Instead, he pet our curls, and went for my sister's with a hand drill. She and I, knowing he was crazy, laughed to see him like that, and bent our heads close. But the drill was real in his hands, and it bellowed for a target. Angry, it sputtered. Until, probing its long tongue into my sister's hair, it seized a strand-- the color wound out of her with it. She screamed and so did I before my father got the drill off the boy. Afterward, the streetlamps clicked on and the boy was next door, having supper, when I rubbed my thumb over the bare patch on my sister's head. All summer long, I drank red cokes with the fellas, ankle-deep in our creek, best hair on the block.

The Local Boys

The boys were smoking Black and Milds around our hedge
and laying odds on first string soccer.

Mikey said the new kid's father
died in a car accident last year.

It wasn't true, Andy replied,
it was the middle of breakfast,
heart attack from nowhere and him,
head in his mashed potatoes, gravy
dripping onto his cold, dead thigh.

Davy had just come in from kick-arounds, the first
cold wave of the year, and his cheeks were red
when he cried for his mother.

Mikey told Andy
that no one had potatoes in the morning
and Andy told him back
he'd never met a German.

When it rained, the boys used to toss snails at the window.
The idea was to see what stuck—

The Holding Pond

I asked for a drink and we took it around the holding pond. You talked
about nude modeling with your girlfriend in Bologna
and I wasn't moody on the walk. I even showed you
my new hairy armpits.

We bayed like dogs around the banks of the apartment.
You asked who I'd been to bed with—
It was a slow trick, magic, the sun
caught in our eyes.

But the hare
got stuck. We tried drawing it
from the hat, but it was stuck.

Nautical Astronomy

I left my shift with no excuse.
No moon. I never even said
my feet hurt, and my eyes
were sore without that great light.

I heard an engine turn
ahead, I heard my father
on the radio. Stood awake
in no streetlight, static, in nonsense shoes.
The snow getting in at the ankle.
Everything colder now,
and the little Toyota he had, slowly moving on.

Bad Dog, Come Back

And if you still don't want to talk,
        I'll shove away my yapping jaw.

If the heart's the trouble, it's my big red heart,
        sounding my dreams up the windpipe.

If everything - if it's all
a huge mistake, I'm telling you,
        you said it.

So what if I lost the car keys?
I lose everything. I'm always
        losing something.

If the goose is yours,
        it's cooked.

If the jig is up, no one said so,
        and I've still
got my leg in the air.

        If everything you say is true, everything I did
was lie.

And I never think of Jupiter anymore.
Or drive my car over that long bridge. I never—

Even

A sandwich is left half eaten
in street pack ice.

      Probably just before some boy wizzed
into the river, before

he cried to a girl as he zipped up his trousers
about how beautiful she looked.

Even the lips that pulled hot from the bread
      went cold in that winter snooze—

going home

      Drunk.

I Bring The Body To Work In

Everything hangs on the ass, so,
leaving the regulars to their spirits, I pull up jeans
with thumbs through the belt loops and tie the apron
at the smallest part of me. Everything,
even the smallness, is a lesson,
and I keep a list.

I've never seen a careful drunk,
but I've seen the boys playing shuffleboard:
the same checkered shirts, the dicks on their receipts,
the way they are stepping over
that dropped fork again and again—

Item. I lean over, handing out beers,
and the table tries guessing my cup size.
Across the universal, swallowing crowd,
the other waitress looks up from the computer,
some scrap of memory gone—

The boys keep saying
"take note." And I do.

They keep touching my shoulder,
calling me baby.
Like I like it.

Who's the Bitch

So who's the bitch now? And what's she got under
        her fingernails? And where has she been digging?
        She listens to the news when it's the woman she likes.
        Late, in her orange kitchen, she moves her nudie body

to the Moody Blues, has three cats, eleven toes.

On the phone to her friends, she says:
        I just want my guy to take me down
        under the sheets, on a small boat, in the Caribbean.
        I just want my guy with a good head of hair
        and maybe, a little family money.

In the morning she keeps having,
        he water moccasin beats her to the nest box,
        is fat with her eggs when it hisses—

In the dream she's awake for,
        her foot is pinned to the gas,
        she's losing all her teeth— ping!
        ping! ping!

Everyone knows
        she's cold wearing that.

So she's cold. What else?

Shall I tell
        about her body,
the way it looks
when she's low?

One Last Thing

Your almost-full pickup
as it is beneath my pressing hands. You
getting under my skin again,
turning me red.

The boxes, all taped and marked—
and soon, a darker patch where you were on the driveway.
Old girl,
churning its silver breath as it moves away.

Our faces like they used to be on the dashboard,
the features easing out of shape
after all the sunlight,

taken once the cold water
in Useppa changed our hair,
chasing the dog who fought the current
and turned, sloppy-tongued.

His empty maw a pound
of angelfish, of sea water--
photogenic.

Sea Witch

Got in late tonight and, by the light
left on in the bathroom, watched the drunk
going home spin wet pirouettes.

And then I thought of you.
You, and that call you made, wasted
from your mother's old phone; how
we used to bake fishies in clay and bake them
until we could flake all of the earth away.
And we had the body in a bowl; a full meal.

Breaking the bones, we hummed Don Rich.
We used a dull knife.
We used our bare hands.

Back then I thought you were Ursula when beautiful,
trapping the things that swam,
sewing scales to your purse.
Such a thing to believe! I can't believe
I felt that.

But then, tonight: watching the old hag
fall over her bad knee, curse
the empty street. The last of her beer
gone. I thought that was you
on your hands, looking for your voice.

Me, in bed,
quiet and cool.

I'm Telling You Ma

Everyone was really looking at me when I first blew into this town; as if I were more beautiful and tragic than that huge oak we kept long as we could, till it had to be cut down, or else lose the house in some hard, tropical breath. The manager, he took one look at me in my kitten heels and said I had to be Jacqueline Kennedy; he found the run in my leg and said Oh, married me, and stayed quiet when I faced the city head on. Yet when I put on my best lipstick, really put it on for the first time in forever--on that day, people all over the bar kept on crawling, chewing their sandwiches, desperate for the Patriots. My lips, painted with painful dedication, checked again in my driver's side mirror, could've been anybody's; I was no new bird no more. So I got the mirror out of my pocket and showed it to the sun. And even when I took my own loofah, and polished all the dingy parts of me till I smelled of warm vanilla all the way to my underneath, nobody took notice, or moved their mouths at me. I even looked at the gnarly old dishwasher and tipped my chin, to say, "Go ahead, pinch my ass!"

Suddenly, the day was over. The hour for rolling around back seats in big leather boots, finished.

I was a beauty once, ask anybody! Today I smile, and bat my pretty eyes at the no good, dirty rotten hound dogs, but they've moved on to tip better-feathered birdies.

When I Go Down

When I go down I'll have been a woman,
        so use my fists for things
better than potting dandelions. Lay me
        in a swimsuit in the snow—
my body will turn blue & lovely & the whales
        will sing lonely, a song for me.

When I go down sew your name on my palm
        with red yarn— marry me.
My garland will grow between elbows of ice
        & wet hair & then call me queen.

When I go down fetch the linen from my pocket,
        tissue scraps, jean thread,
press a thistle in & then stuff it all
        into my mouth.

That filling I've been needing can nestle
        something that's crying,
gone from its nest. If you put me near an ocean,
        let the eels gather

between the rooks, hatch children in my armpits.
        They will practice
catching me in flame. Give my body
        to the peat soil then,

let some dog root around my face,
        some sculptor bury her
lovely hands in my ribcage again. Forgive me

if I stay. My hair you can have if you'd like it,
        so long as you promise the blackbird
a tendril to stuff his nest. In death, even,

I'll say that I'm sorry. Break my knuckles if that will stop
        you from cracking yours. Take them
with you, to give a good squeeze

when you're feeling
        hard-pressed.

Homecoming

He brought me here in his mouth.
Back, to the very end of the cul-de-sac,
which curves, like the grey old lips
of the manager counting up my bills.

Now comes the birth; one thousand
points of darkness
in a closing bar to sink my nails into.
Out of his back: breakfast,
an egg to crack till it bleeds and eat myself
when he's gone. The grass

is only long here, the scraped
summer knee that catches and never heals.
The night pulls, escapes.
And the fingers I wedged in panic
to touch the house key.

I catwalk in a blue bedroom
like a calf getting its legs, screeching,
in love or hungry.

My lipgloss can glow in the dark,
but I lower my breath
when he feels around for me

and we all disappear
whenever I shut my eyes.

My deepest gratitude to the editors of the following publications in which these poems originally appeared:

"Eve Shovels A Grave", *Aurora - The Allegory Ridge Poetry Anthology, Volume 1;* "Upon Hearing Dragonflies Fake Their Own Deaths to Avoid Males, I Consider Wendy Peffercorn", *The Jet Fuel Review, Issue 17.*

I am forever indebted to the minds and hearts who leant themselves to me and to my poems:

Paco Fiallos, David Rivard, Mekeel McBride, Charles Simic, Samantha DeFlitch, Morgan Plessner, John McDonough, Becca Van Horn, Katie Brunero, Ann Williams, Tom Payne, Ciara Lepanto, Chris Boley, and Alex Driver. Thank you to my beautiful, patient family, Mom, Dad, Rhiannon, Carys, Celyn and Clint, without whom this book would not be possible. Thank you to Justin Glazebrook for believing impossibly in me.

Thank you to Freddy La Force and all of Vegetarian Alcoholic Press.

Thank you, Kate Divoll, whose guidance graces me, and whose drawings kill me.

www.ingramcontent.com/pod-product-compliance
Lightning Source LLC
Chambersburg PA
CBHW030142100526
44592CB00011B/1014